'What is Bitcoin'

The Beginner's guide to understanding Bitcoin/Cryptocurrencies, the underlying Blockchain Technology and ways how people monetize the Cryptocurrency trend

Dr. Abhishek Sanoria

Copyright © 2012 Dr. Abhishek Sanoria

All rights reserved.

ISBN: 9781790655410

DISCLAIMER

'What is Bitcoin', The Beginner's guide to understanding Bitcoin and other Cryptocurrencies, develops the reader's fundamental understanding into the new emerging field of cryptocurrencies and Blockchain technology. The guide addresses some basic questions about cryptocurrencies, ICO's, the fundamental technologies and develops a strong base for an average reader to understand this trend and its possible implications. It also equips the reader to become a part of this trend by clearing some basic questions on how to get started.

The advice given herein, and the knowledge shared however, in no way should be taken as an investment advice, or a registered advisory service and the readers should take their own independent decisions whether to engage their investments into this new technology. The guide's sole purpose is to develop a basic level of understanding and clear out some major questions for people who are very curious about this technology and at the same time need a one place solution to develop this learning. In no way, this should be considered an investment advice, or the strategies listed here as a fool proof method for monetizing this new technology. The cryptocurrency world is very turbulent and might cause a big/complete loss of money if entered without proper knowledge.

The guide gives the readers a solid starting point to building their essential knowledge into this new technology and creates a fundamental base, through which, readers are enabled to do their own independent research and decide on their options to pursue this as an option to put their money into. The author clearly highlights the risks and pitfalls associated with this technology and is not liable or anyway responsible for the investment results.

Contents

The Bitcoin Craze 7

What is Bitcoin 12

Blockchain basics 18

    Wallets and Transactions on a Blockchain network 25

Smart Contracts 30

Wallets and Bitcoin storage 32

Blockchain for businesses 36

    The 'Blockchain' benefit 38

Altcoins 47

    Ether/Ethereum (ETH) 49

    ERC- 20 tokens 52

    EOS 54

    Tron 56

    VeChain 58

Ripple (XRP) 60

Litecoin (LTC) 62

Bitcoin Forks 64

Private coins 72

Monero 74

Dash 76

Monetizing cryptocurrencies 1: Investing 78

Monetizing cryptocurrencies 2: Trading 84

Monetizing cryptocurrencies 3: Investing in ICO's 102

Token Air drop 109

Token Burn 111

Monetizing cryptocurrencies 4: Cryptocurrency mining 114

Bitcoin mining hardware 118

Cloud Mining 123

The Trader's words of wisdom 124

The Bitcoin Craze

Bitcoin, one of the largest trending topics across the internet in the last year, has gained tremendous attention from one and all. It has also emerged as 'hope' for the people struggling with their 9-5, to make a big buck and escape the rut. There have been several stories, YouTube videos etc. flying around the internet showcasing rags to riches stories about guys having nothing previously, moving around in Lamborghinis, thanks to Bitcoin. Bitcoin has soared from its value of almost nothing to almost 20,000 $ at the end of 2017, making it a dream for beginners such as 'Sam' to catch this train of excitement. Sam, like many others, is looking for a route to escape this monotonous 9-5 schedule and wants to find solace in Bitcoin.

The 'What is Bitcoin' beginners guide, shares the story of Sam, an average employee living in the outskirts of New York and trying to make it big, through Bitcoin and other cryptocurrencies. Sam, just like every other neighborhood guy works his butt off every day making ends meet and saves some money which he plans to invest and turn into something fruitful, fast. This wishful and ambitious thinking made him consider several options where he could park his savings and ideally multiply them manifolds. He brainstormed into traditional methods such as investing in gold or property which have slow returns. Starting a new business was also never something Sam was skilled at.

Stock trading was not seen as option for him either. When he thought about stocks, he was always afraid of competing with the big investing firms which have tones of money at their disposal and utilize the help of several algorithms to read deep market insights. This gives them a technical edge over a beginner such as himself, who has no clue about predicting market trends and utilizing them to his benefit. Succeeding here would mean beating the massive algorithms trying to churn out market trends for the big investment firms. The stock markets are also impacted by these firms which can influence their movement, especially for smaller stocks.

After the stock market crash in 2008, when Sam was kicked out his first job, the confidence Sam had in the stock market dwindled. Sam being a bit ambitious, wanted to make a quick buck and with the stories of Lamborghinis aplenty on the internet, he was wondering that this might be his chance to make it count. As its said, it is 'never too late to try', Sam started to look for more knowledge into the elusive world of Bitcoin. Being extremely busy at work the whole day and having zero technical knowledge, this sounded very challenging. Sam, had a great boss who was extremely skilled at writing emails and always kept Sam on his toes. Still, he was hopeful about this new technology, believed that it holds promise and started to build his knowledge bank about 'Bitcoin'.

With a very strong grit and determination, Sam took to the internet to join the Bitcoin bandwagon but alas, he was surprised! The internet was alive with Bitcoin and the more Sam looked for information, the more he was feeling lost and confused. He tried and learnt, did not relent but ended up spending an enormous time into gaining useful information about the field of Bitcoin and cryptocurrencies which he put together as the 'What is Bitcoin', The Beginner's guide to understanding Bitcoin/Cryptocurrencies, the underlying Blockchain Technology and ways how people monetize the cryptocurrency trend'.

The journey Sam went through in the Beginners' guide would help any average 'Sam' go from zero to a decent level of understanding about Bitcoin and other cryptocurrencies. He would thus be enabled to understand the Bitcoin concept, the underlying Blockchain technology and its possible applications. He could also make his first purchase and even start trading or investing in Bitcoins. At the end, Sam takes you through his entire journey, still not having manage his Lamborghini, but a big wealth of Bitcoin knowledge for the many Sam's out there. He also shares four possible ways of cashing into the crypto craze, that he learnt while making several connections along his challenging journey through Bitcoin.

What is Bitcoin

Sam was eluded by the name, Bitcoin. Is it a coin that I can put in my wallet, or is it like swiping a card in the bakery for my morning breakfast? Who decides its value and is it safe as an investment option? The more he thought about all these questions, the more he was curious to learn. At the same time, all these interesting questions made him a bit unsure on where to start. Thus, he started out on understanding the background of Bitcoin, how it came into existence and why is it pitched as the currency that could supposedly change the world.

Bitcoin or any other cryptocurrency is a digital asset, does not have any face value as such and is more like a digital currency. This was historically created in 2008, when Satoshi Nakamoto released a paper online titled: Bitcoin: A Peer-to-Peer

Electronic Cash System. It is still not clear who exactly is Satoshi Nakamoto, whether it is a person, a group of persons or a company who developed the concept of Bitcoin and released the open source code of Bitcoin. This could even be Sam's long-lost childhood friend who lost contact with him after starting his own tech startup.

After its initiation by Satoshi Nakamoto in 2008, Bitcoin slowly gained more attention and more people started to get their hands around this new technology. It was around 2013, when Forbes declared this as the year of Bitcoin. Bitcoin started to gain massive interest from Investors, which propelled the prices of Bitcoin even higher than Gold (ounce) during that time. The Bitcoin price went up to over a 1200$ which was just over 12$ a year ago, in 2012. This meant a massive surge of over 10,000% in a timeframe of just a year. Such an increase was unheard of, or even imagined in traditional investment or trading strategies. Thus, this new technology gained a lot of attention. This later broke all records in early 2018, when its value reached over 20,000$.

Bitcoin surpassed the price of 20,000$ in 2018, but still there is a difference on how its value is determined compared to Fiat currencies such as US$ or Euro €. Fiat currencies such as the US$ are a legal tender issued by the government, which maintains its value. Bitcoin on the other hand is not controlled by any government and its price depends on the market value i.e. controlled by the demand and supply of Bitcoin. The more Bitcoin gets mainstream and its demand increases, the more its price is likely to go up.

But hold on, does that mean we can buy something with Bitcoin? Currently, there are only a few places which accept Bitcoin as a currency for buying stuff but the number of shops/ platforms accepting this as a medium of exchange has seen a decline due to the price volatility of Bitcoin which has nosedived again from almost touching 20,000$ in Dec'17 to a little around 8,000$ in April' 18. The price volatility and the transaction fee on small purchases made it non-attractive as a means of exchange among merchants. Nonetheless, the technology being in the nascent phase, still has come merchants offering goods such as gift cards, pizzas etc. accepting

Bitcoins. The mass consumers are mostly unaware of the technology and the payment systems still being a bit uncertain, have curtailed its rise in terms of mass adoption.

Nevertheless, the real essence that Sam could get out was, that Bitcoin has still not developed itself as a full-fledged technology for replacing the current methods of payment. But he was still wondering what caused the price of Bitcoin to soar up to 20,000 $ and how would he be able to realize his dream of making it big with cryptocurrencies?

The demand for crypto assets comes generally from investors who are currently seeing them as investment options, believing that their demand would further soar once the technology is up for mass adoption. Currently, only a small proportion of the world has heard about this new technology and from these, only a tiny fraction really understands what it is. This leaves many people like Sam who wish to be early adopters and gain as much as possible out of it, while the technology is still in the growing phase. Bitcoin, cryptocurrencies,

Blockchain and crypto trading are just a few of the several areas which have seen meteoric rise in online content. Many trading platforms have come up and, there are tons of success stories of early Bitcoin adopters making it big.

Before trying to understand a bit deeper on how these success stories have been possible, it is essential to get a deeper understanding on the underlying technology.

Bitcoins and cryptocurrencies use cryptography to create, verify and authorize transactions. A popular word used in context of cryptocurrencies is that they are 'decentralized'. This sounds like a heavy word but what it essentially means that there is no central institution which has control of Bitcoin. For example, all Fiat currencies such as the US $ are controlled by the central government, Bitcoin on the other hand has no central institution controlling it. How this works is through a technology called the 'Blockchain' which is like a public transaction database, synonymous to a distributed ledger, which relies on a decentralized infrastructure. What this means, would be covered shorty.

Blockchain basics

Blockchain, as Sam would put it, it is like a continuous list of online records which keep on growing. These records are called as 'blocks' which are linked to each other and include the timing of the transaction taking place together with the transaction data. This network of records called the Blockchain is managed through a peer to peer network for validation of each transaction. Once recorded on a Blockchain network, it is extremely difficult to alter the transaction as this would require altering the entire peer to peer network where it got validated and stored. Therefore, it is also referred to as a decentralized, distributed and public digital ledger. The meaning of each of these terms would be explained later. A Blockchain, can be envisioned to be something like a network of connected blocks of data as shown the below.

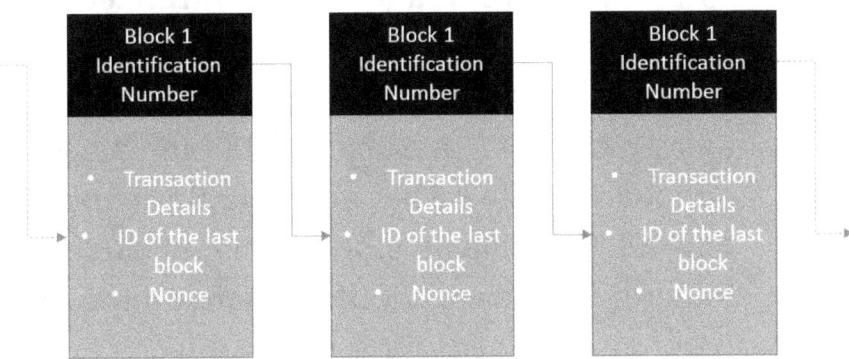

The record 'blocks' which store the transaction data, are linked to each other and carry the identification number of each of the previous block. Each block has also something called as a 'Nonce' which is essentially an arbitrary number used in cryptographic communications to make the blocks secure. Each 'secure' block is linked to the previous block, storing its ID and thus forming a chain, thereby getting the name 'Blockchain'.

The prime difference between Blockchain and a physical ledger used by Sam's grandfather to maintain a list of his financial transactions is

A) **The Blockchain ledger is decentralized:** This means that there is no central record of data unlike Sam's grandfather, where, he locks away all his personal data in a secret cupboard. Only he has access to this cupboard and all the data is stored only in one place making it centralized. Blockchain on the other hand is managed via a peer to peer network where the data is stored across several systems. So, let's assume that Sam's grandfather goes on a holiday and there is a fire in his apartment during this absence.

He returns safely but finds out that his apartment has been destroyed by the fire, which also gutted down all his personal data. There is no way for him to recover this data which now stands lost forever. This is the major drawback of having data stored in a centralized location.

Centralized data sets are often vulnerable to theft, pilferage and destruction by unforeseen agents. The Blockchain ledger on the other hand is not stored in one central location, this means that even if one location where the data is stored gets destroyed or is rendered nonfunctional, the record is not lost as it stays at multiple locations. Breaking into such a system to get this data becomes even more difficult when the locations can be located anywhere across the globe and on any computer. This makes Blockchain technology extremely difficult to break through or steal information from being 'Decentralized'.

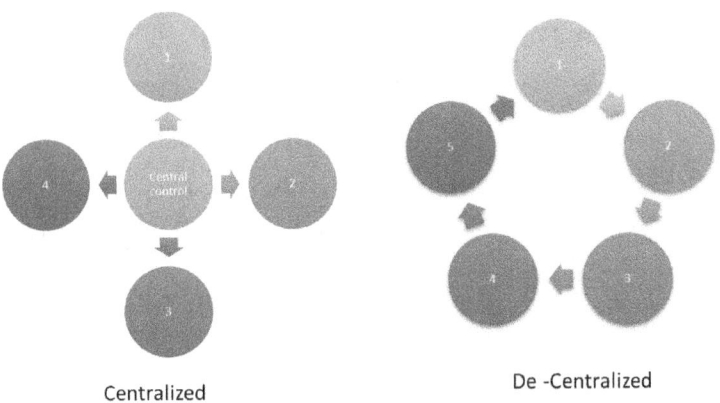

Centralized   De-Centralized

B) **The Blockchain ledger is distributed:** Data recorded on a Blockchain network is encrypted and coded as a 'block'. These blocks of data are linked to each other forming a chain thus the name 'Block chain'. The information added through each block on the Blockchain has a special code which is accessible to anyone. Thus, it is possible for anyone to check if this information is correct and it is distributed across the Blockchain network. These networks are called as nodes, forming the backbone of the Blockchain network.

These nodes or computers/devices forming the Blockchain network are responsible for storing and adding information to the network. Any computer or device such as a phone which has internet access can be a node. It can then just maintain a copy of the Blockchain or/and process and add blocks to the network. Adding information as explained above means putting them into blocks and adding it to the Blockchain, often called as mining.

Thus, a block been mined on the Blockchain essentially means that the information being stored is accepted and added to the Blockchain ledger. However, processing and adding these blocks to the network requires high computational power. Due to this, mining through a mobile device is generally not effective and would only cause loss of time without any significant return.

C) **The Blockchain ledger has a digital signature:** Coming back to the example of Sam's grandfather again, he always used a lock to secure his records. Only he had access to this lock and no one else could open it, without him giving his key. Of course, there were always some experts in breaking locks and stealing away his records. In Blockchain, data security is maintained through digital signatures. The digital signatures secure the transaction through the Blockchain database and is a way to prove the authenticity of a person on the Blockchain. This also ensures that the person is not a hacker or someone who is trying to modify the information contained through the Blockchain network, the digital signature being unique.

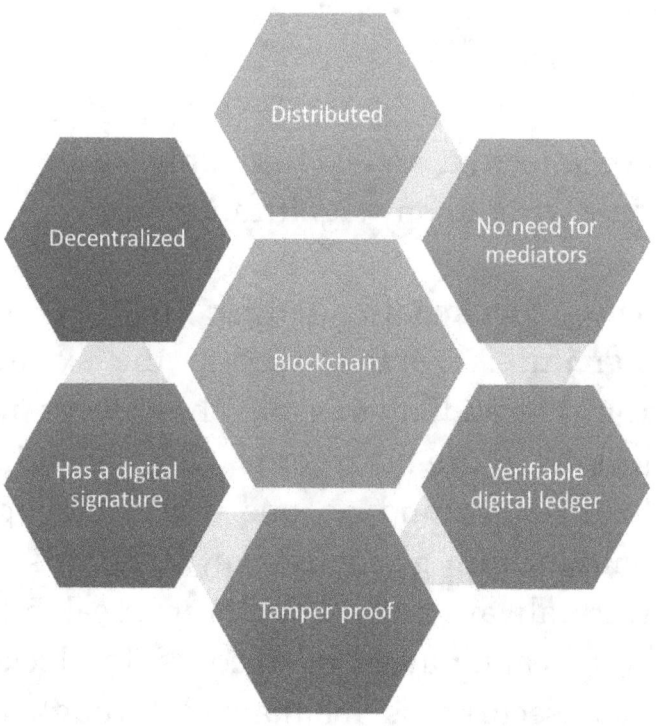

This validation of transactions taking place through the Bitcoin network is called 'mining' or Bitcoin mining. The Bitcoin miners get a return for their effort in validating these transactions and this return is in the form of the cryptocurrency they are 'mining' or validating the transactions for. How mining takes place and, how could it possibly be used to earn money would be covered in a later section.

Wallets and Transactions on a Blockchain network

Transactions on a Blockchain network happen once it is initiated from a user and then validated by the Blockchain network. Validation means that the network verifies that the right transaction is happening, the information/ currency being transferred is available with the person sending it and it is delivered to the correct delivery address. Essentially doing the work of a middleman in a transaction business. For example, in businesses such as banking, share transfers, real estate etc. the whole industry is based on a middle man or multiple middlemen who help carry out the transactions.

The buyer often does not know the seller and the trust in the transaction comes from the middlemen for which they generally charge a large amount of money. Middlemen are often biased and add unnecessary complexity to the system. This is where Blockchain helps as it is simple, unbiased, cheaper and fully transparent.

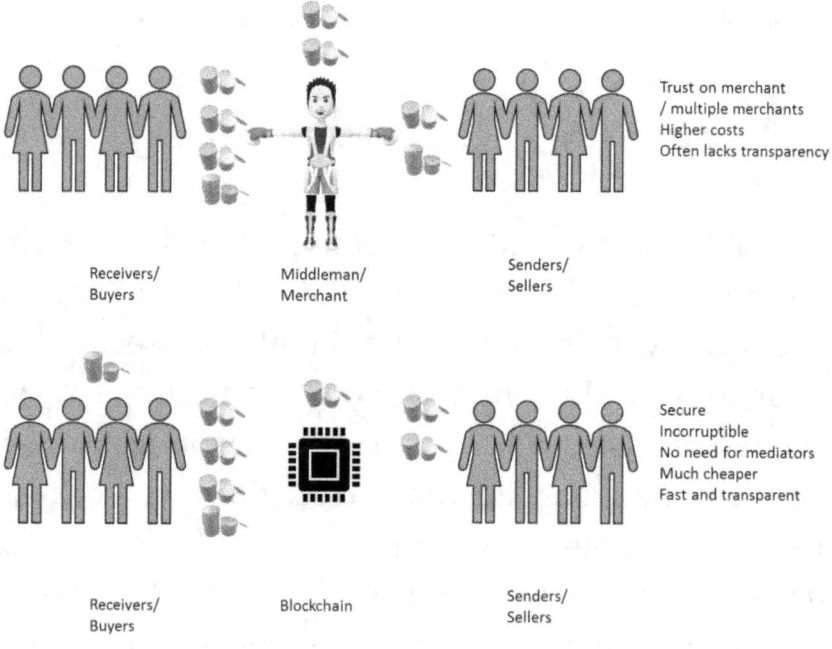

As seen, the amount of money which trickles down to the middlemen for the transaction becomes very less. On top, the added amount of trust and transparency that Blockchain brings in is enormous. The saved money resides with the buyers who get a service which is automated and free from bias/manipulation. Thus, Blockchain technology has a huge potential of disrupting traditional Businesses, which involve several middlemen who often bypass a lot of money through the transfer.

But how are these transactions happening through a Blockchain? Transactions happen through a Blockchain network by creating a digital address of the person carrying out the transaction. This digital address keeps a record of all the transactions happening for that certain person on the Blockchain network. A long list of characters comprising of letters and numbers such as below forms the digital address.

8HmeKAJ9nNsahKKnjHmK J7JJsz8NiUnb

The digital address comprises of two types of addresses also called as 'keys'. One is a public key, which can be accessed by anyone and a private key which as the name describes is meant to be kept private. The public key is 32 characters long whereas the private key consists of 64 characters comprising of letters and numbers.

A very important point to note is that, even by mistake if the private key for a user is shared with someone else, then he can transfer or divert the contents of his Blockchain account to any other account. However, the public key can be shared with anyone and is used for all transactions. Here, it is safe to assume the magic of the Blockchain technology that, even if everyone knows your public key, it is nearly impossible to find out your private key.

A bit more details on the transaction process is as below. Let's assume Sam wants to transfer some Bitcoin to his friend. What would happen is that, the Blockchain network would verify if Sam's account has the amount of Bitcoin he wants to send over to his friend. Sam's digital signature which is his private key would be used to create a digital signature which would be used to sign off the transaction. This digital signature would confirm that it is indeed Sam who has carried out the transaction.

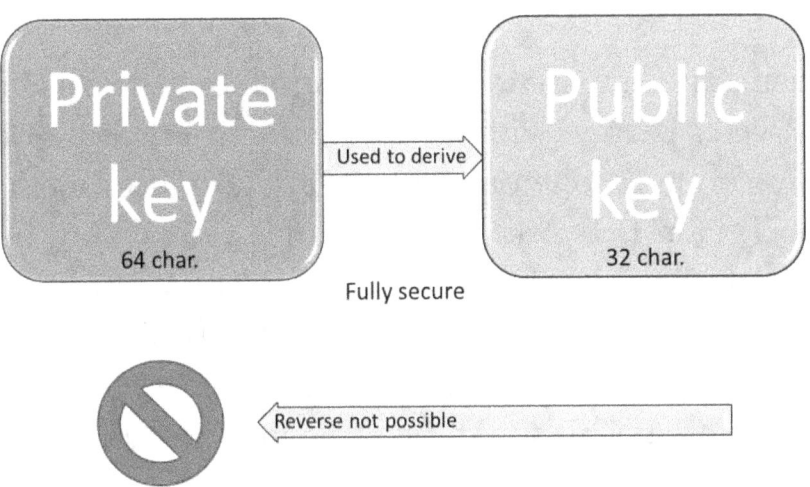

The private key is then used to create a public key and coupled with the transfer sum and network information which is used to transfer the Bitcoin Sam wants to transfer to the receiving address. Even though the public key is created using a private key, the vice versa is not possible. This is a one-way route and thus is secure.

Smart Contracts

Blockchain being decentralized allows direct business transactions/ information exchange between parties without middlemen. But how do these transactions or exchanges take place on the Blockchain network? This is enabled by setting up decentralized self-executing contracts on the Blockchain called 'Smart Contracts'. These are self-execution enabled contracts and execute based on the terms specified in the smart contract code.

Being decentralized, the supervision of these 'execution terms' is carried out by the network of nodes or computers linked through the Blockchain network. This brings the tamper proof benefit of Blockchain and the contracts exchange money, or anything holding value for which the contract has been setup. The terms and transactions are recorded permanently on the Blockchain network and the identities of the transacting parties remain confidential. These 'Smart' contracts or Digital contracts often run on 'If-Then' principles i.e. 'if' a certain criterion is met 'then' a service is executed. For e.g., if the payment of a certain commodity being sold is received 'then' that commodity e.g. shares or tokens are released.

Wallets and Bitcoin storage

While giving the example of a digital signature on a Blockchain network, we had mentioned transferring Bitcoin from a wallet. So, what's a Wallet when we talk about Bitcoin and other cryptocurrencies? The Bitcoin wallet or any other cryptocurrency wallet stores your private key which allows having access to your funds. As mentioned previously, if one gets access to your private key, then he can gatecrash and siphon off your assets. Therefore, it is very important to secure your Bitcoin wallets to avoid any threats of losing your digital assets.

Generally, there are three different types of Wallets available

a) **Software wallets:** Software wallets are applications which store your public key securely online and display the number of Bitcoins/ Cryptocurrencies that you have in your account. With the wallet, you can do transactions with other wallets and store your assets safely. The private keys during transactions are handled by the application which is a trusted third party such as, several exchanges which list this service online e.g. Coinbase. There can often be another added security layer such as two factor authentications added to the wallet, which would be enabled while accessing or making transactions through the wallet.

Software wallets can also be of two subtypes namely: cloud based, or desktop based. A cloud based wallet is where your information is safely stored on a cloud network or can also be directly installed on your computer. These wallets generally have the advantage that they can be accessed from multiple devices and locations. The desktop wallet on the other hand can only be accessed from your private computer or device where it is stored.

b) **Hardware Wallets:** As the name suggests, hardware Wallets are devices which store the private key or the 'Wallet' for the cryptocurrencies and connect only sometime to the internet majorly during transactions. The hardware wallet software provides a public key to the network when a transaction needs to be completed and this way, the private key is kept safe from any attack by hackers or any online vulnerability. Some of these even come with a display which makes it easier to track the contents of the wallet and keep a track on transactions. Popular companies providing such hardware wallets include Trezor, Nano S etc.

c) **Paper Wallets:** A document printed on paper holding your public and private keys for transactions is called a paper wallet. The paper wallet often has the public and private keys stored in the form of a QR code which can be scanned easily when you wish to make a transaction. These can be created using websites such as Bitaddress.org etc., which would generate a random public and private key which can be then printed on a sheet of paper. The advantage of a paper wallet is that it is completely detached from the internet and there is no chance of any hack or malware attack as there is no interface with the internet. Still, while printing the wallet it needs to be ensured that the printer is not connected to the internet to ensure full safety. The big negative of having a paper wallet is that if the paper gets lost or burnt/ damaged etc., there is no way to recover the keys back and the crypto assets would be lost forever.

Generally, if you intend to use Bitcoin or any other cryptocurrency for transactions, then online software wallets would be the most convenient wallet to go for. If you are looking to store your crypto assets more a long-term investment point of view, then a hardware or a paper wallet may be the more viable option for you.

Blockchain for businesses

So, a secure and reliable distributed public ledger is the essence of what a 'Blockchain' is but, what is it good for? How does the whole world of cryptocurrencies surround this technology and what are its possible applications, that we hear every other article around the internet talking about the next revolution in technology being 'Blockchain technology'.

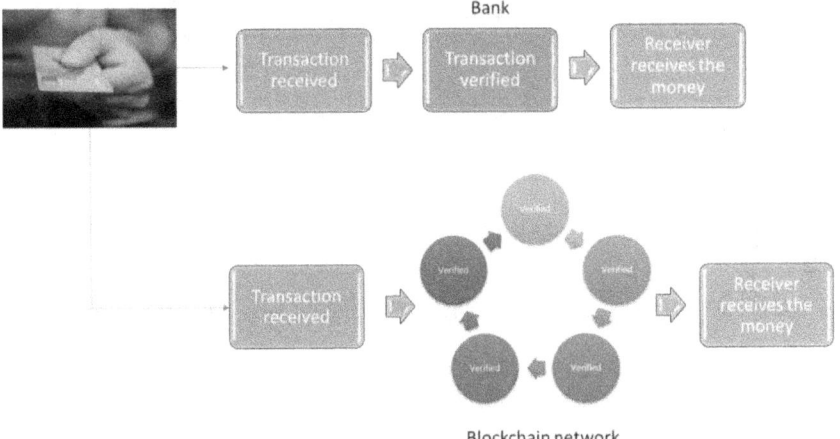

Let's imagine you use your credit card to order something online. The transaction is verified through your account by the bank. There needs to be sufficient funds in your account for the transfer and the details of the account you wish to transfer the money to, should be correct and verified by the bank too. Using Blockchain technology, this happens through the Blockchain network, where the network verifies the transactions and if the network agrees then the transaction takes place. The network verification means that using Blockchain technology, there is no need of a mediator or a middle man for verification and the records for transaction stays in multiple entries.

The 'Blockchain' benefit

Blockchain as mentioned above being a secure and decentralized system has a big advantage that it allows validation of ownership of a ledger entry which can be a digital asset, in a public manner. What this means is that if there is a record which exists on the Blockchain network then it 'stays', it cannot be tampered with and manipulated. This record also comes with a time stamp which makes it even more valuable. Imagine a dataset to which you can only append information which cannot be altered with. The possibilities of such a technology can be enormous especially in areas where this information is managed by mediators. There is no longer a need for these mediators and more importantly no need to pay them for their services.

Let's take an example of explaining this better. Sam gets down the airport and needs to drive to his hotel. He arrives late at night and has no other option apart from taking a taxi. Previously, he used to go to a taxi booth and order a taxi for which he paid a commission to the tour and travels company. This commission was generally around 20-40 % of his ride and the rest went into the drivers' pocket. Mobile booking, which has sprung up recently like Uber and several other companies made it easier for Sam to book his taxi online and reduce the cost by doing away with the direct mediator.

The mediator in this case is the company e.g. Uber, which provides Sam the service of helping him find a ride back home. Uber here is partially decentralized where; the data and the transaction is controlled by Uber. Blockchain technology takes it to another level by making it completely decentralized and the control of the entire transaction rests with the user. In this case, Sam can book his ride through a 'cryptocurrency token' and the driver can be paid in this token itself. Where this helps essentially is when, let's say Sam is in Lagos where US$ is not accepted.

Paying in cryptocurrency would allow him to pay directly without having to worry about the currency exchange rates and he can also maintain a permanent record of his transaction on the Blockchain network. There is also no third party such as an application or a taxi provider which would eat into the commission on his ride. Thus, his ride would be cheaper, the transaction transparent and its permanent record would be maintained over the Blockchain network automatically. There have been several trials of such taxi services enabled through Blockchain technology e.g. Tada, which has shown successful trials in Singapore.

Similarly, Blockchain technology can provide people control over their finances, their data and make transactions more transparent. Through this transparency and permanent nature of transactions, there are several industries which can benefit from this, such as supply chain, logistics, marketing, healthcare etc. Another example of the benefit of Blockchain technology is in data creation and record maintenance.

Let's assume Sam meets up with a good friend David, who is a scientist and together they invent a new drug which has the possibility to eradicate a deadly disease from the face of Earth. Now, Sam and David are not the only people developing this drug. They know that there are many more people working in the same direction to find a technical solution around developing this revolutionary drug formula. Both now want to file a patent on this drug, but patent filing takes time, involves preparation of a heavy list of documentation and not to mention the hassles of finding a lawyer or a patent filing agency.

Sam was busy preparing these documents and finding a patent filing agency. But, this preparation and sorting out the legal framework took him some time. While doing so, he found out that his competitor in China, also working on the same technology knew the legal framework a bit better. He made a similar technological breakthrough and filed his patent earlier than Sam. This meant that Sam could lose his technological edge that he would have gained, having discovered his 'formula' first in the world and having solved a major consumer need. This is where Blockchain technology would have come in handy. Sam and his friend could have maintained a record of his technological breakthrough on a Blockchain network and this record being indestructible, would have stayed with a timestamp of when the record was made. This could then be used by Sam and his friend to claim a patent on this new discovery.

Another example where this can be useful is maintaining a record of new artwork, images or creations which can be easily copied. Let's assume again that Sam does a crash course in sketching and starts creating brilliant sketches which make him very famous. He then opens an art gallery where he starts selling his artwork creations. Now, his artwork having a novel abstract theme becomes very popular. As the demand for Sam's original sketches rises, counterfeiting and copying begins. A consumer willing to spend money on this very new abstract art form wants to purchase the original sketch. Art is often bought as an investment and thus Sam's popularity would be hurt tremendously if the buyer cannot track the authenticity of his artwork.

Blockchain technology would allow Sam to maintain a record about his creation and this can easily be verified by the purchaser who wishes to buy it and ensure its genuineness beforehand. It can also easily track 'when' Sam had created that piece of artwork.

Similarly, Blockchain Technology has a tremendous promise in ensuring anti-counterfeiting and authenticity in several good and artifacts such as antiques where the value of the item is in its really being original. A few industries seeing the tremendous potential of Blockchain technology are as below.

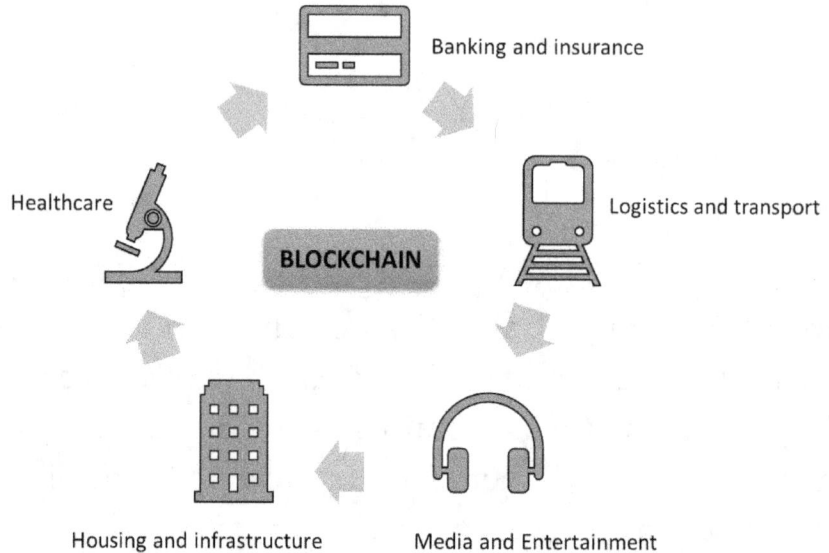

Apart from these, Blockchain technology can also be of great relevance in the consumer goods industry to track authenticity and gain more information about the products. Tracking the authenticity for raw materials/parts could also be a big boon in manufacturing to prevent counterfeit goods entering production and effecting final product quality.

Walmart, one of the largest multinational retailers is working with IBM Blockchain solutions to develop a Blockchain solution for the food industry. As reported, before using Blockchain technology it was very difficult for Walmart to track their source of food in the stores. But with Blockchain technology, this tracking time can be reduced drastically from weeks to just 2.2 seconds! This becomes very helpful in instances such as a disease outbreak e.g. E Coli. The infected batch or batches could be easily identified and prevented from reaching the consumers, thereby curtailing the spread of the infection. Walmart is planning to expand this further to ensure food traceability and security to its consumers.

Enough talk about the underlying technology and Blockchain in a nutshell. Sam was now looking for the more interesting information on how he can get his hands on his first crypto asset and possibly start making money diving into crypto technology.

Before making the first investment into Bitcoins, there is another important term which needs to be understood in the context of cryptocurrencies, called 'Altcoins'. Altcoins stand for alternative coins. Bitcoin was the first cryptocurrency and by far the largest in terms of market capitalization. There have been several other cryptocurrencies launched later which are called as Altcoins. These Altcoins are generally improvising further upon the issues faced by Bitcoin or starting a new concept of transactions on their own Blockchain network.

Altcoins

Bitcoin is not the only cryptocurrency in the market as mentioned, but the first and the most dominant one, controlling the entire cryptocurrency market. After Bitcoin, there have been thousands of Altcoins which have been launched and this number keeps on growing every day. Most of these Altcoins try to improve some aspects of Bitcoin or try to solve an existing issue in the market. These

Altcoins are based on the similar underlying Blockchain technology but designed in a different manner. Some Altcoins are just catering to a niche where the Blockchain technology could be a gamechanger such as in storage of medical records etc.

There are several important Altcoins which, together with Bitcoin dominate the cryptocurrency market namely Ethereum, Ripple and Litecoin etc. Interestingly, new coins such as Bitcoin cash and EOS have replaced Litecoin as the number 4 cryptocurrency but where this list stands in the future is anybody's guess. New Altcoins keep on coming up improvising on the existing technology of the current coins. The bigger the promise in terms of the technological advancement over an existing coin, the bigger are the prospects of this new Altcoin replacing the current one.

Ether/Ethereum (ETH)

Ether is also an open source, Blockchain based cryptocurrency launched in 2013. Ether is based on an operating system called 'Ethereum' on which several altcoins/ Blockchain based technologies can be created. In Sam's words, Ether is created on the Ethereum platform. 'Ether' as said, is generally referred to as the cryptocurrency based on the Ethereum platform. But for many more beginners in the crypto world, when talking in trading cryptocurrencies, generally both terms refer to the same Ethereum based cryptocurrency.

The basic idea of launching Ethereum was to create a scripting language to create other crypto applications. The currency was created based on this scripting language to improvise on certain aspects such as low transaction speed of Bitcoin. The transaction speed for Bitcoins was essentially 10 minutes which was reduced to around 15 sec. with Ethereum. The transaction fees were also reduced significantly which made the market cap of Ether soar to become the second largest cryptocurrency currently.

Bitcoin, being a cryptocurrency only tends to solve the challenges in the financial domain and disrupt the banking system, Ethereum on the other hand aims to disrupt the internet by offering a platform for creating several Apps (also called DApps or Decentralized Applications). Apps created on the Ether platform would offer the user more control of its data as it would not be managed by a third party and instead be managed by the Blockchain based,

Ether network. Again, all benefits of the Blockchain technology while doing away with third party based apps. The data is stored on the secure Ether network, which is decentralized, and the owner has full rights and control of his data.

Recently, there has been a huge rise in the number of new applications being launched on the Ethereum platform which also raises a big question about its scalability and its ability to sustain them. The scalability factor is a big question which is very difficult to find the answer as, all these technologies are still in the nascent phase. Where the future of such technology would be in the coming years is anybody's guess but the technological concept is indeed very promising.

ERC-20 tokens

While we talk about Ethereum, a very important term which often comes across is ERC-20 tokens. As said, the Ethereum network allows support of building more decentralized apps which utilize the Ethereum Blockchain technology and upgrade it with the application they wish to cater to. The transactions on these Dapps happen using the Ether currency and the network contributes the necessary computing power for running these applications. These applications might create their own tokens which can be sued for trading or utilizing the applications and since they would be built on the Ethereum network, they are called as ERC-20 tokens.

There is a small limitation with ERC-20 tokens that the transactions can only be made in Ether as the currency and if some other currency is used for this transaction then the tokens might be lost forever. There have been several very popular Altcoins or ERC-20 tokens which have been built on the Ethereum platform such as EOS, Tron, VeChain etc.

EOS

EOS is a cryptocurrency token launched mid-2017, which also allows to generate smart contracts and build decentralized applications on the EOS Blockchain network. EOS was created to try and solve the issue of scalability within Bitcoin and Ethereum networks and increase the transaction speeds tremendously. EOS was previously created to run as a decentralized application on the Ethereum network. It later implemented its own Blockchain network called EOS Mainnet, giving it the capability of having decentralized apps being built on its network, separate from the ERC20 network. The tokens being held previously on the ERC 20 network on the Ethereum network migrated smoothly to the new EOS Mainnet network.

EOS also aims at eliminating the transaction fees for users through a special algorithm. The block time with EOS was reduced to 500 milliseconds compared to around 15 seconds for Ether and 10 minutes for Bitcoin. Currently EOS is in the top 5 cryptocurrencies based on market cap.

Tron

Tron is another Blockchain based cryptocurrency which was launched in Sept'17 with the aim of decentralizing the digital entertainment industry. With Tron, the idea behind was to serve as a protocol for creation of a free entertainment ecosystem, where the content creators e.g., someone creating their own song or video over the internet would have full access to interact directly with the viewers/consumers. They would be fully in charge of its circulation, storage, publishing and earning revenue from the digital assets created.

Tron also allows for creation of DApps or decentralized entertainment applications on its network. Tron had started off based on the Ethereum network but slowly migrated to its own Mainnet network mid-2018. The Tron network's token is called Tronix or TRX.

VeChain

VeChain (VET) was launched much earlier in 2015 and started based on the Ethereum ERC 20 tokens. It later developed its own Blockchain network just like Tron and EOS. VeChain implements a smart contract-based platform which helps in inventory tracking. It is focused on internet of things and supply chain management solutions which diversified lately into financial management solutions. Vechain combines its Blockchain technology with smart chip IOT solutions enabling tracking of goods, foods, luxury products and ensuring quality enhancement for products.

It aims at creating more transparency in the system since the quality of the goods in the supply chain can be tracked and ensured end to end. It also ensures that the authenticity is maintained and can be tracked, the Blockchain network being tamper proof. Luxury goods is one of the major beneficiaries of such a concept as there is a huge amount of fakes floating around for luxury products such as watches, bags etc. and sometimes it is extremely difficult to track its genuineness which could be tracked through VET. Recently VeChain has rebranded itself into VeChain Thor and is still in the top 20 cryptocurrencies based on market cap.

Ripple (XRP)

Another cryptocurrency doing the rounds and dominating the internet space is Ripple. This was initially released in 2012 and is one of the top five crypto currencies in terms of market cap.

Ripple is described as a basic infrastructure technology for interbank transactions and a neutral utility for financial institutions and banks. This allows financial and non-financial institutions to use Ripple as a medium to offer its consumers their services. Ripple is backed up by two transaction entities namely, the regulated financial institutions which holds and issues funds on behalf of customers. The second being the trading desks providing liquidity to the consumers for the currency they wish to trade/spend in.

While looking on the internet for Ripple, Sam always stumbled into the worlds which resonated multiple times 'Ripple is controlled by banks' whereas Bitcoins and other currencies wish to do away with the banking system. This is what it means. In Ripple, the currency requires a regulated financial institution such as banks which control the transactions.

Till date there are 100 billion ripple tokens which have been created and this is a big number in comparison with Bitcoin and Ethereum. This is also a reason that even when the value of ripple is below 1 $, it still holds a significant chunk of the crypto market cap.

Litecoin (LTC)

Litecoin was once among the top 4 cryptocurrencies which has now been replaced by newer cryptocurrencies such as EOS and Bitcoin Cash, still Litecoin has a substantial market cap and holds relevance among crypto enthusiasts. Litecoin was created with a goal to improve upon Bitcoin and essentially uses a different algorithm compared to Bitcoin, which makes transactions on the Litecoin network significantly faster than transactions on a Bitcoin network.

The faster block generation in Litecoin enables a double confirmation in 5 minutes which would need at least 10 minutes per confirmation of transactions with Bitcoin. The average block mining speed in Litecoin is 2.5 minutes compared to 10 minutes for Bitcoin. This enables many transactions to be carried out per day with Litecoin compared to Bitcoin. The faster block generation also means that opportunity to earn mining rewards with Litecoin are higher compared to Bitcoin. Litecoin also has a coin limit of around 84 million compared to 21 million tokens for Bitcoin.

Bitcoin Forks

Another important term which often comes across in the cryptocurrency world is called as 'Forks'. This is essentially very different to the stuff that Sam uses to finish off his lunch every day. A fork used for eating scrapes off a portion of Sam's plate allowing him to eat whereas, a Cryptocurrency fork acts a network divergent which breaks down the Blockchain network into two or more parts. There are two relevant definitions of a fork regarding cryptocurrencies. The first is when a Blockchain diverges into two different paths and the second refers to a change in the protocol for an existing Blockchain. Generally, forks are created to add new features to an existing Blockchain network. This leads to creation of two separate versions of the Blockchain which carry the same history.

Forks normally happen just like a system upgrade on your personal computer. Cryptocurrencies and their inherent Blockchains like any other technology incurs an upgrade to offer feature upgradation. Once this upgrade occurs in a Cryptocurrency let's say to increase the block size or increase the number of transactions, a 'fork' gets created.

Generally, there are two types of forks which are created namely a 'hard' and a 'soft' fork. A hard fork means that the upgraded path or new functionality added to the Blockchain causes a split in the Blockchain path and a new path or cryptocurrency is created. A 'soft' fork is when only the newer version of the cryptocurrency or the upgraded Blockchain version remains, essentially adopting the new upgrade.

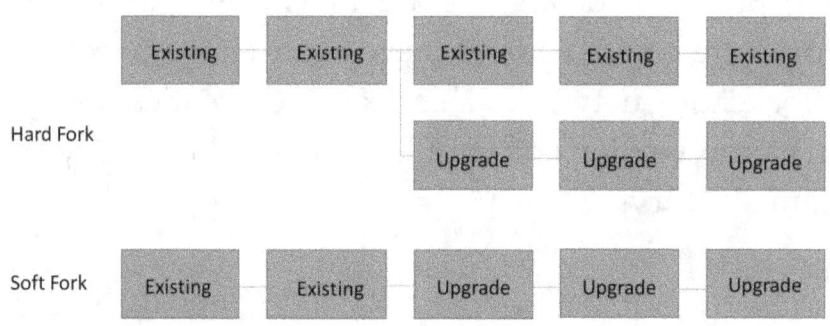

Till recently, there have been three Bitcoin hard forks created, which are now very popular Altcoins as below

1) Bitcoin Cash
2) Bitcoin Gold
3) Bitcoin Private

Bitcoin Cash

Bitcoin Cash or (BCH) sprung out of Bitcoin as a hard fork on 1st Aug'17 making it a recent Altcoin. BCH was created to increase the block size on the Bitcoin network from the existing 1 MB to 4 MB. This would eventually lead to an increase in the number of transactions which can be processed on the Bitcoin ledger. As Bitcoin Cash was created, both the original Bitcoin Blockchain and the new BCH existed together. The good thing when this split occurred was that anyone owning Bitcoin was automatically entitled to gaining the same number of BCH tokens as well. Bitcoin Cash enables sending money across the globe with minimum fee, all around the clock.

Bitcoin Gold

Bitcoin Gold or (BTG) was created as a hard fork out of the Blockchain ledger to improve upon the mining functionality of Bitcoin on 24th October'17. BTG essentially could be mined effectively with graphic processing units (GPU's) or computer graphic cards instead of using sophisticated mining equipment used in Bitcoin mining. This makes it easier for anyone having standard laptop with an installed graphic card to obtain BTG. This is enabled by being based on a separate algorithm instead of the algorithm fueling Bitcoin. Again, anyone owning BTC was entitled to automatically get the similar number of BTG tokens. Having said this, BTG was hit by a massive hacking attack in 2018, stealing money from several exchanges where it was listed on.

Bitcoin private

Bitcoin private or (BTCP) was created or forked out of the Bitcoin ledger more recently in Feb'18. BTCP was essentially a merge fork created out of Bitcoin and another Altcoin called Zclassic. Bitcoin private as the name suggests has the additional functionality of keeping the identity of the sender, receiver and the amount of transaction private when a transaction takes place. This was completely opposite to BTC where the transactions are completely transparent. The users can exchange funds without leaving a trace of their history.

Private coins

Bitcoin and many cryptocurrencies encrypt the details of a transaction but still being distributed and verifiable, the public key can be seen by anyone. This means that the value of each transaction as well the balance in the wallet can be seen by anyone. The public address of the sender and receiver, both are visible. Sometimes these details might be secret, and some companies or institutions would like to keep these anonymous. There might be trade secrets or simply details of large transactions which someone or some companies who do not wish to divulge them. To solve this challenge, there are a special class of cryptocurrencies called as private coins which keep these details secret as well but at the same time maintaining the decentralized nature of cryptocurrency transactions. Some of these cryptocurrencies include, Monero and Dash etc.

Monero

Monero is a private cryptocurrency created in August 2014, which uses a special 'obfuscated' public ledger for transactions. This means that the details of each transaction over the Monero network such as the source, the value or the amount of cannot be viewed by anyone. They have a separate mechanism for mining and validation which still ensures the benefits of the Blockchain network. Every transaction happening on the Monero network is carried out by generating a stealth address which is like a onetime public key. The receiver receives the funds not directly to their wallet but, through this stealth address which is validated like normal cryptocurrencies. Due to the stealth addresses, it is not possible to divulge the details of the transactions. Owing to its complete anonymity, there is a high chance that private coins such as Monero can be used by antisocial elements for transactions.

Dash

Dash is another cryptocurrency which was forked from the Bitcoin network in 2014. It started with a name called 'Xcoin 'which was later changed to 'Darkcoin' and then, to its current name 'Dash' in 2015. Dash provides two additional capabilities compared to the Bitcoin network namely private transactions and instant transactions. Dash aims to create a digital currency which is decentralized, secure and easy to use. It works on a special algorithm called InstaSend which facilitates instant transactions on the Dash network. The Dash website also calls it out as Digital Cash you can use anywhere and thus the name Dash.

Sam was now overwhelmed with these new technological developments and had obtained a decent level of understanding about the cryptocurrency world, the Blockchain technology, several of the major cryptocurrencies out there and the problems they wish to solve. Due to his limited understanding about the underlying codes and digital technology, he was quite satisfied with his overarching understanding of the crypto world. He now wanted to make his first move into understanding on how to jump onto the crypto wave and this exciting new technology. He was looking to be one of the early adopters and generate tangible value from being amongst the first ones to do so. That's where he entered looking for ways on how people earn money through crypto assets.

Monetizing cryptocurrencies 1: Investing

Investing into Bitcoins/ Altcoins or purchasing Bitcoin as a long-term investment option is the first strategy used by several people who believe in the technology and its value increasing even further as more and more people adopt the technology making it mainstream. Ultimately, the value of these assets is determined by demand and supply.

While choosing investing in cryptocurrencies as an option to reap benefits from its possible future growth, there are several options to do so. Many online platforms or cryptocurrency brokers available these days where it is very easy to invest and store these cryptocurrency assets.

US based consumers generally prefer platforms such as Coinbase, Bitstamp, Binance and Bitfinex etc., whereas for consumers based in Europe, Bitpanda, Bitstamp etc. are popular and convenient platforms to make your first crypto invest. For consumers based in China, Japan and Korea there are several other exchanges such as Coinmama, Kucoin, HitBTC and BitFlyer etc., which are very popular.

Recently several trading platforms such as Markets.com, Plus500 and Etoro etc. have also started listing cryptocurrencies. All platforms offer the purchase of not only Bitcoins but other Altcoins such as Ethereum, Litecoin, Bitcoin Cash, Ripple and several others. Based on market volume and trade, the top 3 are still Bitcoin, Ether and Ripple which dominate the large chunk of transactions happening through the crypto channel.

It might be possible that if you are looking to purchase a certain altcoin such as IOTA etc., these might not be able to be purchased directly via a platform and you might have to purchase Bitcoin first and then get this converted into the Altcoin you are looking forward to purchasing. This gets done at the current value of the Altcoin against Bitcoin or whichever cryptocurrency you wish to make the exchange.

While purchasing his first crypto assets and trying to establish his portfolio of 'tokens', there was a slight hurdle which Sam was getting annoyed with called 'KYC'. KYC stands for 'Know Your Customer'. It is a legal process used by business entities to identify their clients. Several websites for purchasing crypto assets have an extensive verification process which might involve giving several of your personal identification documents and still involve further verification through a video chat interface. Yes, you heard it right, verification through a video chat to confirm your identity. This is because Bitcoin transactions cannot be easily tracked to the user and can be used for illegal purposes. There are strict regulations from governments to block this loophole and prevent illegal actions such as money laundering. Thus, these online platforms make an extra effort to secure the user's identity before granting him complete access to bigger investment in cryptocurrencies.

There was an added feature that Sam was prompted to implement for his account to ensure multilayer security, apart from choosing a strong password. This feature is called as 'google authenticator'. Basically, this is an app that you can download on your mobile phone and sync with your cryptocurrency platform. While logging in your account, there is a code appearing on the app which you would be prompted to input.

Only once this code is verified after entering the correct password, you would be able to successfully enter your account. This makes breaking into your account extremely difficult as someone would have to know your password and your google authenticator code at the same time to get into your account for causing damage. The google authenticator generates such codes randomly every minute and making a guess is virtually impossible. All your wallet or cryptocurrency accounts can easily be linked to the Google Authenticator app and while logging in next time, you would be prompted to enter the code generated for the linked account through the App.

After going through the tedious procedure of verifications and securing his account, Sam was finally able to login securely. He was now ready to setup his cryptocurrency portfolio and make his mark, hoping to cash in on the next crypto surge such as the one happening beginning of the year taking the world by storm.

Monetizing cryptocurrencies 2: Trading

Having made his first investment into the crypto world, Sam was feeling that he needs something more and still his dream of owning a car with doors opening vertically seemed a distant vision. The crypto portfolio he had built was seeing a stagnation in value, as in the last few months, major cryptocurrencies had seen a slide rather than a surge. Investing and waiting for the cryptocurrencies to reach mass adoption or the market demand to create a second surge seemed ambitious. With the future being uncertain as it is volatile in the crypto world, Sam was looking for something more.

That's when Sam met a good friend Tom, on a lovely Friday evening, sharing a table in an after-work party. The two guys were sitting all alone and started chatting up, where Sam opened to him on his new-found interest, cryptocurrencies. He realized that Tom was involved very closely in the same. The conversation became very interesting when he told him about the money he was making every day. Sam was a bit shocked as he thought that investing in the crypto world would help him make his mark but, barely moved the needle in his favor and how could Tom make money every day!

After a few more drinks and a bit of friendly persuasion, Tom started sharing his secrets. He was trading cryptocurrencies and making money from the huge daily fluctuation in price that the Cryptocurrencies were going through. A few more drinks made him confess that he was not always in the green, but overall the amount of money he made was higher than the amount he lost. Tom attributed this to his knowledge about the trading market, knowledge about sources to track these fluctuations and of course his 'stars'. Sam was till startled about this new way of converting his crypto portfolio into profit and he started digging deeper.

Tom, now being in a long friendly conversation, started to advise Sam into crypto trading and how to monetize the dips and rise in the crypto market. The huge volatility in the market is the key to making money. But starting with just a little bit of money in the bag, how could you trade a higher volume was Sam's question. Tom smiled and replied that the secret there is called Margin Trading.

Margin trading

Margin trading allows you to trade several times the money you have and keep the profits you generate on the bigger invest you make. Sounds simple, but there is also a flip side as if you incur a loss then the loss would also be amplified. Margin trading can be explained like borrowing money from a bank. Let's say you have 1000 € and the bank offers a margin of 10x which means that it offers you 9000 € as a loan. Now you can trade on this total value of 10000 € instead of the 1000 € you had initially. Let's assume that you made some spot-on trades where the value of your trades go up by 10%, then you make a handsome 1000 €.

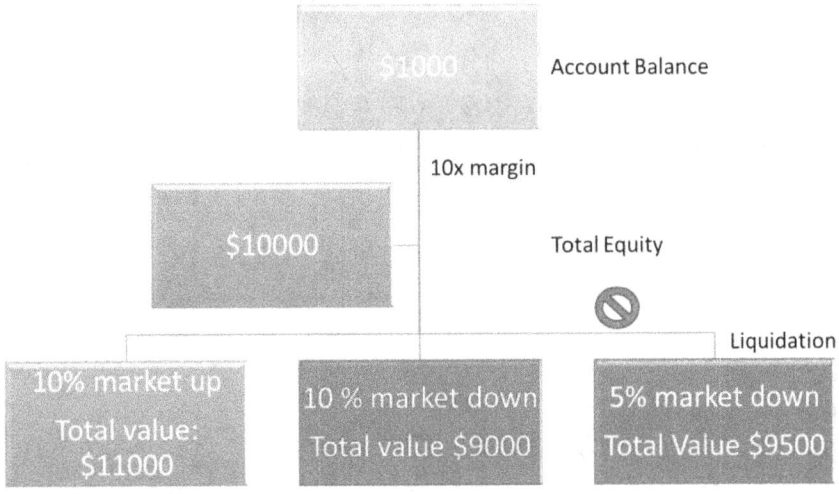

But, if the market drops 10 % you already lose all your initial investment and must cough up some interest on the 'borrowed' money. Generally, platforms allowing margin trading, limit the amount of loss your account can take to 40-50 % of your account value. The trading platforms have a right to sell of your assets in case your loss falls below this number of 40/50 %. They generally issue a warning notification when the value of your assets fall below 60/70 % and this warning is called a 'margin call'.

When receiving a margin call, it is advisable to close off some of your open positions rather than losing them all when your account falls below the 40/50% range. This is called 'liquidation' and you would lose all/ partial of your trades to ensure you do not lose more money than that you have put into your account.

The assets being closed depend upon the trading platform and they generally have full right of closing some or all your open positions to recover the loss. This makes margin trading extremely risky as a sudden market movement against your trades can render your account being liquidated and you ending up losing all your money. Thus, margin trading is extremely risky and is not for the faint hearted, as it might result in wiping out of your entire account balance extremely fast.

Still, there are several watch outs which need to be considered while trading esp. on margins ads these can have a big impact on the market fluctuations.

a) *Market knowledge*: The first and foremost thing about margin trading is market knowledge and the parameters governing it. The crypto market is influenced by a huge number of parameters which, for a beginner like Sam would be very difficult to decipher. But there are several things he should be aware of and use it to his benefit.

The regulations in the Bitcoin industry are one such big watch outs. In February' 18, there was strong message given against cryptocurrencies by the Indian government where they clearly mentioned that they do not consider these having any monetary value. This, with a few more such negative news had a negative impact on the cryptocurrency prices causing a bearish run in the crypto market. There are several tools which can be used for keeping a track of crypto news daily being

     a) Cryptonews.com

     b) Bitcoin.com

     c) Cryptocompare.com

     d) Coindesk.com

     e) Ccn.com

f) News.Bitcoin.com

g) Blockchainnews.com

These are only a few of the many channels available online where Tom used to increase his knowledge about crypto and kept on following for updates. He advised to follow at least a couple of them regularly for gaining knowledge on the possible rise and falls in the market. Then, use this knowledge for placing an intelligent bet on the trading patterns.

b) *Price Trends:* **While trading cryptocurrencies, another thing to keep into consideration is to identify the trends in the price fluctuation. This can be done by monitoring closely the price variation of the currency being traded. Coinmarketcap.com, cryptocompare.com are some very useful websites to keep a track of the rise and fall in the crypto prices.**

This is also useful in identifying some trends showing the rise and fall of a particular cryptocurrency. Generally, the price of most currencies rise and fall together with Bitcoin leading the race. But, sometimes the rise of one currency is higher or lower than the other.

Crypto A	-10%
Crypto B	-12%
Crypto C	-8%
Crypto D	-15%
Crypto E	-6%

Let's assume the above case showing a bearish market scenario or a market going down. Here the entire market has seen a fall but interestingly the value of Cryptocurrency E has fallen lower compared to A. Which essentially means that Crypto E has risen in value while compared to A. This could be used as a pair for trading for a rising trend for the A/E pair if we can make a strong assumption that the Cryptocurrency E is stronger withstanding the lower trend.

Therefore, this relative rise or fall could be monetized with a careful market watch and predicting trends in price fluctuations.

c) Hedging and minimizing losses: **The biggest watch out that need to be taken care of while margin trading is, to never put all your eggs in the same basket. The fluctuations in the crypto market are enormous and sometimes even a very watchful trend analysis, coupled with a market watch might leave you with your trades on the opposite side of the prediction. To avoid this uncertain situation, it is always advised to maintain a portfolio of investments in several coins rather than just placing all your bets on a solitary option.**

There are two important trading terms which are often used to describe where the markets are heading. These are, a bullish (bull) market which essentially means that the markets are going up and the stock price or commodity price is going up. The other is a bearish scenario (bear) which on the other hand means that the markets are going down and the price of the commodity is dropping. When the market is uncertain on where it would be heading, it is always an option to put a bigger trade in the direction where you are more certain and a smaller value of the trade in the direction opposite. While, this might lower your profit earned if your market assumptions are correct, it would hedge your loss if the market goes completely against your predictions. To understand this a bit better, there are two more terms which are important to be understood while trading i.e. going 'long' and short' in trading.

Going Long means buying a share or cryptocurrency when the market is showing a bullish trend and is expected to grow. When you go long on a share 'x' then you expect that the value of this share will rise with the bullish trend you have identified in the market. Going short on a share means the complete opposite. Let's assume that Sam invests a 1000$ in cryptos A and B. He sees a strong bullish trend in the market and expects the price of crypto A to rise significantly because crypto A was just listed on a big cryptocurrency exchange and had come into big partnerships with several firms. Also, the market trends were strongly bullish and thus Sam went long 800 $ on crypto A.

A few hours passed, and some negative news came about a hack in a cryptocurrency exchange in Japan. Now, the bullish trend became a bit weaker, but Sam had full confidence that his trade is in the right direction. Still, he is not completely sure as no one can predict the markets perfectly. Thus, he decides to short 200$ in another crypto which he feels might face the brunt of the trend reversal to a bearish trend. Doing so if the markets turn against him completely, Sam would minimize his loss. This also would eat into his profits if the markets continue the bullish trend, but it is a risk which Sam was willing to take as what matters is that overall Sam should make money.

The crypto market is a very difficult one to predict and thus hedging is an excellent approach to minimize your losses. Losses in the middle are just a pit stop to the destination moving forward. Unless, you are the real wolf on the crypto street, you will always lose money at some point or another as the markets can be unpredictable at times. What matters at the end is that you should be making money overall.

d) *Learn the candlesticks*: The trading charts (candlestick charts) provide a huge indication about trading patterns. These are the fundamental blocks of trading and can provide a very useful indication about the market movement. Each candlestick typically shows a day but in the crypto market, a day is generally like a decade. Thus, candlestick charts which can track the movement of the market in an hourly or even quarterly basis are very useful. A bullish candlestick is generally in green and a bearish candlestick in red. These are used to identify a cryptocurrency's opening and closing prices in the specific time range and find correlations over a specific time to predict the movement of the market.

Using the candlesticks and trading charts require lots of time, patience and some mathematical skills which need to be picked up over time. There are several good books which can be referred to learn this and several YouTube channels which provide in-depth information about using these charts.

Reading a candlestick is simple but reading the candlestick characteristics and understanding the trends and interpreting them for your benefit is the tricky part. A trading candlestick has 3 basic parts as below.

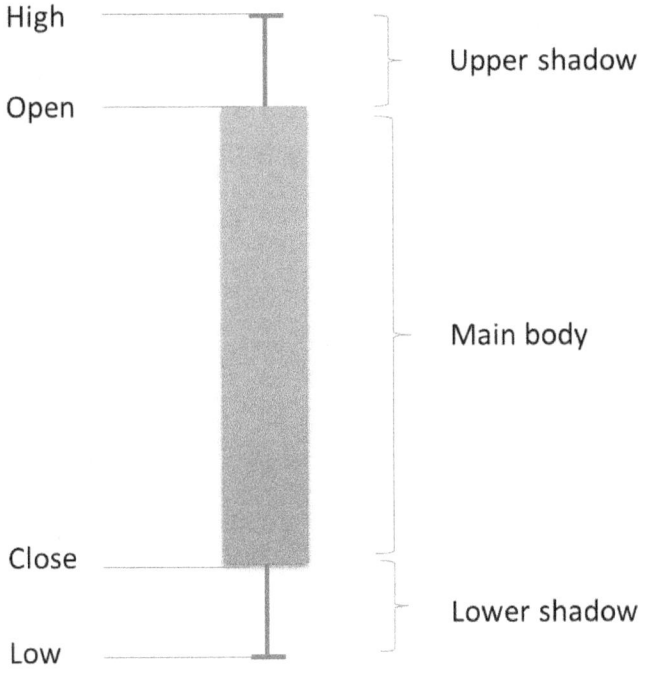

The candlestick comprises of a main body and the upper and lower shadow also called as wicks. The wick illustrates the highest and lowest prices of the traded commodity/ security or in this case cryptocurrency. The body indicates the opening and closing trade in the given duration for which it is being viewed. The relevance of this viewing window depends on the commodity, in cryptocurrencies, this window of relevance is generally a few minutes as the market changes happen extremely fast.

The candlesticks are also of two distinct types as below.

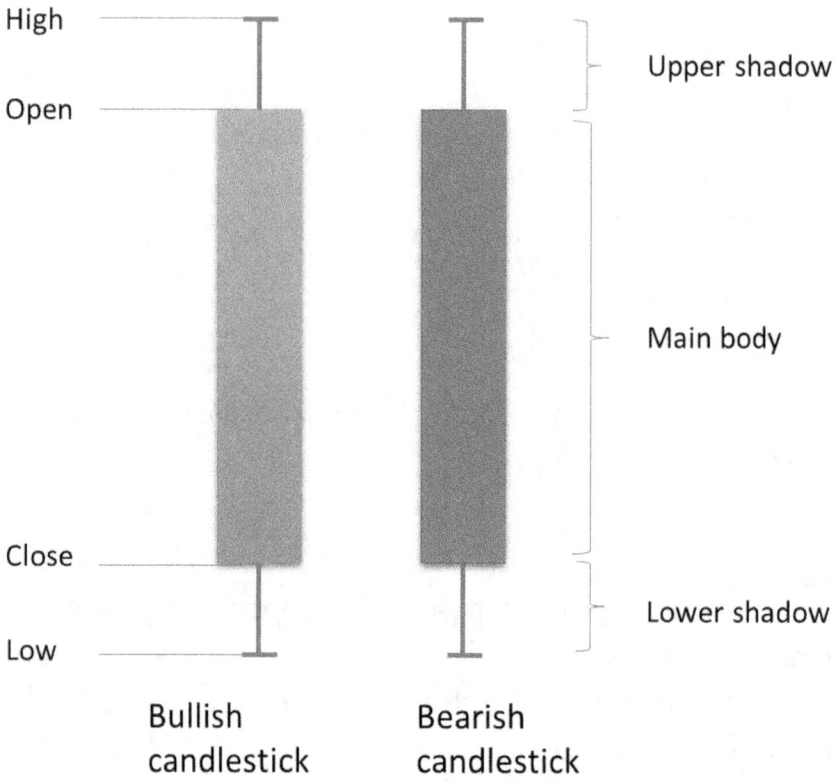

A bullish candlestick is often represented in green and shows that the closing price for this candlestick was higher than the closing price for the previous candlestick. A red or bearish candlestick on the other hand represents that the closing price for this candlestick is lower than the closing price for the previous candlestick. Thus, these consecutive candlesticks line up to form the candlestick pattern through which several important observations can be made about a commodity's movement and a technical analysis can be carried out on future predictions.

There are several good books available on predicting trends using candlestick patterns but there is no perfect fool proof method to do so. It's more learning by doing and the more you try, the more you learn and find your own way of deciphering a pattern. There are several trading channels available on YouTube which also provide more insights into trading analysis.

Monetizing cryptocurrencies 3: Investing in ICO's

ICO's or Initial Coin Offerings, are another option of parking that extra bit of disposable income to earn greater rewards, as the value of the ICO grows with time. But wait, what's an ICO? Sam was a bit startled and it sounded to him like IPO's which mean Initial Public Offerings. An IPO is when the stock of a smaller company is made public to expand their capital. In simpler terms, it is like a company issues its stocks for the first time to the public for gaining larger investment and possible expansion. A recent example of an IPO was 'Spotify', when it chose to offer its IPO to public in April'18 this year.

So, what's the difference between ICO's and IPO'S, are they similar in a way? ICO's are digital assets or tokens on a Blockchain which are sold by a given company in return for cryptocurrencies such as Bitcoin. The essential difference between them is, that issuing an IPO requires the company to showcase years of activity and solid operation for a while. On the other hand, ICO's can be issued without even having a product or a minimum viable prototype. IPO's offer dividends to the shareholders based on profits while ICO's offer tokens to early investors at a lower price with the assumption that the price for these tokens would rise based on the token utility and trust laid into them by the public.

But, how could investing in ICO's possibly generate income? Most ICO's there tempt early investors with a pre-sale option before getting listed on exchanges with a hope of a price rise and with it, the value the investors earn from buying the tokens pre-sale. Having said that, there are some ICO's which solve an existing problem and have a big prospect of growing in the future. Imagine an ICO having a current value of its token at 0.001 $ and Sam invests 10$ in this ICO. Let's assume that this ICO grows to 0.1 $ value in a couple of months, then Sam has already converted his 10 bucks to a mighty 1000$. This is like the Bitcoin pizza story of 2010 where it was said that a guy paid for two pizzas in 10,000 Bitcoins. That time, the value of 10,000 Bitcoins was worth nothing more than 30$

which in early 2018 became over $ 82 million. ICO's if one day become a mainstream technology and if enter mass adoption could see their value surge from their launch or pre-sale value.

Having said that, the ICO market is mushrooming every day and with the lax regulations in the ICO market, it is very difficult to predict which ones would hold value in the future. It might also happen that the money invested into ICO's goes down to almost nothing if the ICO turns out to be a ponzy one and as the majority of ICO's fail, the chances of this are high. Still, there are a few points to consider for guidance while investing in ICO's as below

- **Basics: 'The company website and the legal framework':** It is always advisable to look for ICO's with a genuine looking website and a legal framework in place. The company launching the ICO should be registered in the country where the founders are from and not in a small island nation. Dig into the details of the company address to identify if it really exists.

Generally, all this information is easily available on the company website. A few minutes of google search, about the ICO, its founding members, their history, the ICO legal information etc. can already give some hints about its being genuine.

- Introduction video and the story: One of the most important things to consider carefully is the ICO introduction video on their website. Does it look genuine and trying to address a real existing issue? These days there are ICO'S coming up just about anything and therefore it becomes extremely to carefully assess the story around the ICO. ICO's with a promising concept are more probable to last in the long run. Also, once you have got the concept, try to explain it to a non-tech savvy friend and understand if he got what you are trying to tell him.

If your friend does not get it that means, there is a gap in your knowledge which needs to be bridged. At the end, you only would wish to pledge your money into something which you at least fully understand. There are some ICO's which solve tiny or nonexistent problems or issues and such ICO's are definitely not going to be adopted as a mass, because either the problem is too niche, or they are just a scheme to gather money.

- MVP (Minimum viable prototype) or trail runs: There are several ICO's out there which function with just a whitepaper i.e. a document detailing what the concept is about often too technical to understand for Sam. Whitepaper is a written document which is easy to write as a concept and is generally difficult to understand for a non-techie guy. It is still worth going through it carefully to identify loopholes and if the ICO has already demonstrated a proof of principle. This is sometimes in the form of a trail run or a small base usage called as minimum viable prototype. Without a minimum viable prototype or an app/ trail run, or a very solid concept present addressing a burning need, there is a high change that you might have landed into thin air and no substance.

- Token supply: ICO's offering innumerable tokens have a lesser chance of making it bigger in terms of real value. Let's say an ICO issues 50 Billion tokens having a value of 0.01 $. The value of these tokens is very less likely to blow up to a big value because of the innumerable number of available tokens. This also depends on the problem it is trying to address but unless it is a huge technological breakthrough, solving one of the major problems existing in the world, the value of such a token might only increase marginally.

- Credibility: Watch out for ICO'S being found by genuine looking people. Browse through their social media profiles to determine if these people exist and what do they do. Keep a track of the ICO activity through the social media forums and telegram. Another valuable form is reading blogs and keeping an eye on the social media of the ICO for e.g. Reddit and Facebook.

There are two more important terms one needs to know while dealing with ICO's. These are Token 'Air drop' and 'Token Burn'.

Token Air drop

Token Air drop is a term which is often heard when browsing through new ICO'S during pre-sale. In simple words, token air drop is a very tactical strategy to market the new ICO and provide 'tokens' for free to investors. The investors are free to stock them for future when the token value might go up or even when in future the token is started to be used as an exchange medium for the problem it is trying to solve.

Some investors might also feel that it's a free deal and sell it off on exchanges. Generally, the value of such tokens which are airdropped are quite small. Thus, the value made out from them is generally very less but, it gives the company doing the 'Air drop' a good chance to make their ICO more visible.

What it also does that the people who get these 'Air dropped' tokens have a low tendency to sell or exchange them as the value of these tokens is very less as they are in the nascent phase. This ensures that the tokens stay with the consumers and once the ICO's get their technology ready, their tokens would be up for mass adoption. Generally, Airdrops happen when you subscribe yourself to a certain ICOs' website or sometimes have your account on a certain exchange.

Token Burn

The next and other surprising term encountered often in ICO's is called as 'Token burn'. To understand what this essentially means needs a proper understanding of the ICO listing process.

When ICO's start offering their tokens to consumers, they often set a goal which for them is in terms of the investment they wish to generate from the pre-sale of their ICO. As mentioned earlier, the details about the objective of the ICO and how it plans to achieve them are laid out in a document called as the 'White paper'. The ICO then starts raising funds through presale and tried to achieve its pre-sale target. The ICO's require this minimum investment for developing the technology to bring the ICO to life.

Let's assume a certain ICO was unable to sell the number of tokens it needed to hit its pre-sale target. It can then burn off these remaining tokens which have remained unsold. What it ensures is that there are no tokens which remain having no ownership from either the investors or the company launching the ICO. But how does one 'burn' a digital token esp. a Blockchain based token when we said that what once comes on the Blockchain network cannot be altered with? The way which this happens is exactly the benefit of Blockchain technology.

The tokens to be burnt are sent to an invalid address which cannot be accessed by anyone. Being inaccessible by anyone ensures that these tokens are destroyed or 'burned'. The beauty of the 'Blockchain' network is that this address is easily verifiable and can be tracked by anyone. Thus, the chances of misappropriation are bare minimum as all transactions happening over the Blockchain network are verifiable.

Thus, Investing in ICO'S could be a possible way to invest and possibly grow the extra income. However, it should be kept in mind that investing in ICO's is also very risky as mentioned above. ICO's are like startups in the crypto scene where most of them are destined to not make it to the market and die out even before having a first proof of principle. It is therefore advised to consider the above-mentioned checklist which could be beneficial in making an educated bet before putting your money into ICO's. Having said that there are still some promising ICO's out there which have a solid technology and like a startup, show a big promise of mass adoption once the full technology is ready.

Monetizing cryptocurrencies 4: Cryptocurrency mining

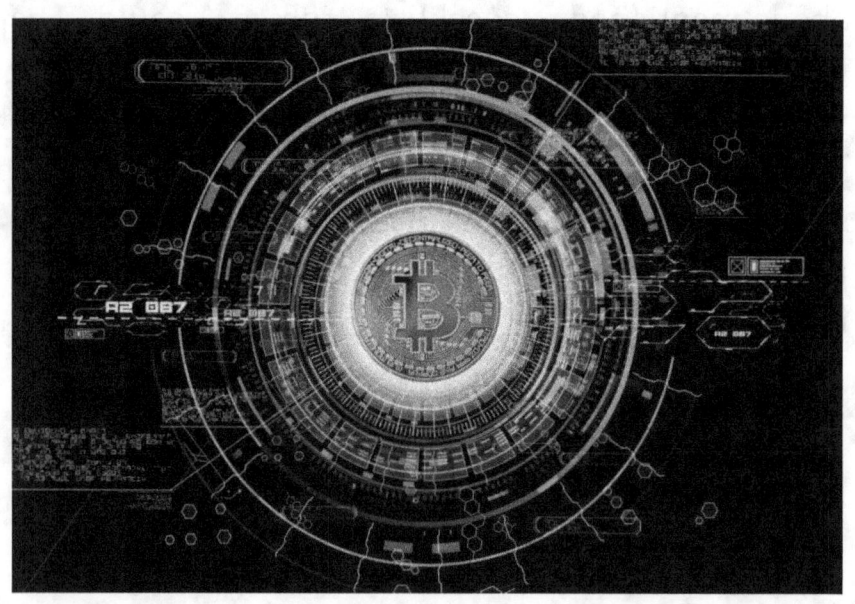

How can one earn money with mining?

More interesting question for Sam was, what is mining in the digital world? If you could recall, while talking about cryptocurrencies such as Bitcoins, each transaction through the Bitcoin needs to be validated. The 'miners' carrying out these validations get payouts in the form of cryptocurrencies they validate, which also includes partly the fee per transaction.

The total available Bitcoins in the market currently, is around 17 Million and the supply limit of Bitcoins is around 21 million. The number of Bitcoins which can be mined steadily decreases as more and more Bitcoins are available in the market. This means that mining the remaining Bitcoins becomes more and more difficult.

The remaining Bitcoins which are existing in the protocol design would be found or 'mined' once the transactions on the Bitcoin network keep getting validated. It is believed that all the existing Bitcoins would be mined somewhere in the middle of 2100 and 2200. But what will happen to the Bitcoin miners then? Still, mid-22nd century is a long way to go and many new technological developments would happen during that time. The answer to the question is that miners earn rewards for validating transactions in the form of transaction fees and the mined cryptocurrency. When all the available cryptocurrency has been mined, then the miners would get the reward as the transaction fee only.

So, Bitcoin mining happens through local computer networks called 'nodes'. The Bitcoin mining software is free and available online through which anyone can turn his computer into a node. These nodes can then link themselves up to an entire nodes network which verify the outstanding transactions on the Bitcoin network and append them to the Blockchain network. They do this by solving a complex mathematical puzzle in the Bitcoin program and then include this answer to the Blockchain.

This is also called a 'hash function', which is the mathematical process which returns the output which can be appended to the Blockchain network. The inputs to the Blockchain or block hash functions are unconfirmed transactions which are written to the Blockchain network through the mining process.

Solving these 'mathematical calculations' requires a very large computational power. Once the nodes can solve them, the Bitcoin network compensates the individual nodes based on the computing power contributed in the transaction process. The higher the computation power, the higher the reward. Nodes having a normal PC would generate rather negligible amount of Bitcoin assets due to the low computational power and end up consuming a very high amount of electricity which is why Bitcoin mining is carried out through sophisticated mining hardware. The mining process sounds complicated but is handled via the mining software and even a guy like Sam can start mining easily once having the required hardware and software installed on his computer as explained below.

Bitcoin mining hardware

The mining hardware capability or power of generating Bitcoin or other cryptocurrencies is often correlated with a term called 'Hash Rate'. Hash Rate refers to the number of calculations the available hardware can perform per second to solve the mathematical puzzle enabling the transactions to be appended to the Bitcoin network. The higher the Hash rate means the more number of calculations can be performed by the miner and the higher chance it has of mining Bitcoin.

One fact which needs to be considered is the power consumption while calculating the possible profits that could be generated from a mining equipment. There are several Bitcoin miners available on the market which consume a different amount of electric power which costs money. This is essentially the reason why Bitcoin mining is more profitable in areas which have cheap electric power.

Bitcoin as said above can be mined from you own personal computer, but the hash rate obtained would be very low. This can be enhanced by using hardware upgrades such as increasing the computational power by adding graphic cards which provide the high end mathematical power as they are designed for this for gaming purposes. PC miners could go for mining Altcoins such as Litecoin which would be much easier to mine via a computer as they run on a different algorithm compared to Bitcoin which is more PC friendly. Still it would be very hard to match the mining capacity of real mining hardware which have a very heavy processing power and receive the biggest benefit from mining.

Sophisticated mining equipment available are in the form of ASIC chips or Application Specific Integrated Circuits (ASICs) chips which provide the right amount of computational power needed to mine Bitcoin. The overall profitability would still depend a lot on the electric consumption and the mining power of the chips.

Bitmain is a company selling several of this sophisticated mining hardware online. Another big drawback with mining apart from the high electric consumption is, the loud noise and heat generated from the mining equipment. Bitcoin mining consumes a lot of electricity and still, even after using a dedicated mining chip, big returns on investment are challenging to achieve. In places which have very high temperatures or in peak summers for eg., the mining equipment might also need some cooling to prevent overheating of the device.

Mining solo generally provides low return because there is a lot of competition and several miners are doing the same with very high computational power. What is another possible option, is to join a mining pool which effectively increases the mining power of your hardware as the combined computational power of the group. This increases the probability of 'mining' the involved cryptocurrency but on the flip side, the rewards generated would be shared across the members based on the computational power computed.

After getting a mining chip or upgrading the computational power of your computer, the first step to getting started mining is installing the mining software available online eg. through Bitcoin.org. This software connects your miner to the network where it receives transactions on the Bitcoin network and keeps track of the Blockchain. The software acts as an interface between your node or mining software and the Bitcoin network.

Sometimes there is an additional software needed to be installed from the mining chip, but this is easy and combined very well with the Bitcoin mining software. CG miner software is a popular program which enables pooled or solo mining. This works well with ASIC miners and is an open source software which works on Windows, Linux and OS X. There is other software available such as BFG miner etc. and mostly all can be downloaded via Github, which is one of the world's leading software development platform allowing easy download of mining software.

Cloud Mining

Could mining is also an alternative where there are several companies which offer cloud mining capability. What this means is that the miner can purchase cloud mining contracts at one of these companies which would do the mining and return the earned cryptocurrencies to the users in return of a profit. This eliminates the additional hassle of purchasing mining kits, spending electricity and verifying transactions. However, the returns if any on these, are extremely slow. The payback is also in the form of the cryptocurrency that you mine and the amount of return would depend on the value of the currency when the contract ends. Generally, the contracts offered run for a year, which is a long wait to see returns from the fast-paced crypto market. There are several frauds also going along with Cloud mining and thus it should be done with an extra mile of caution.

The Trader's words of wisdom

After the huge wealth of knowledge shared by Tom, Sam was extremely excited to take his crypto plunge and asked him one last question.

Should he go all in and realize his dream? The crypto world is booming and with a bit of luck he can make some decent money.

That's exactly where Tom paused him and said. 'Luck' as you mentioned in the crypto world can be very deceptive. The market is **extremely** volatile and in such a volatile market the most important thing to know is when to get out. You need to have a strategy where you should decide what you are after. For doing it, the first step is understanding the technology and then taking your own educated guess about it being a gamechanger or a hype.

The next step would be to decide whether you are considering a longer-term investment strategy or a trading strategy where the risks associated are higher and ending up with a complete loss of your crypto portfolio is easily possible.

When going for the investment option, it would be a good point to start considering which cryptocurrencies would be worth investing into. Is it the traditional, top cryptocurrencies by market cap. that you are looking to take the plunge in or is it one of the more recently launched ICO's which have not gained much attention.

It might also be the case that you opt to have a portfolio of investment, which consists of more known and popular cryptocurrencies and then putting 'some' money into new or promising cryptocurrencies which are solving an existing problem. This would again depend heavily on your financial condition and the amount of risk that you are willing to take with your hard-earned cash. There is no perfect strategy but any strategy which you develop would have the base being your knowledge and risk with this new emerging technology. Of course, this would be governed by your financial status as well. There are stories of people selling their entire house and investing into cryptocurrencies but, as Tom suggested, this would rather be an extremely ambitious idea and a very easy one to becoming homeless.

The other part is when you decide to be a bit more risk taking and try your hand at trading. Trading gets a bit more challenging where in depth knowledge of trends and the market becomes increasingly important. It is these trends and fluctuations which would help you monetize your assets. Thus, it is important to learn and track your sources of information such as popular forms, blogs and news sharing information about latest developments in the crypto field which might have an implication on the market.

While trading, there would always be days which are 'green' where you earn money but this can be followed by a big crash. Therefore, just jumping into trading without a strategy and knowledge would mean riding your luck and taking a plunge into the uncertain. In Tom's language, this is what he called gambling. Gaining information, developing your strategy and sticking to it what he called a planned approach to 'trading'. There are a few points again as below which Tom mentioned which would help minimize losses and reduce the luck factor in trading cryptos as below:

a) **Start small:** The first and most important advice for people like Sam who have no clue about this new technology wave and wanting eagerly to reap benefits out of it would be to start small. Start with something as low as 100 $ and get a feeling for the basic structure on how to buy, how to open a wallet, how to trade etc. and learn the entire process. Try to make some gains with this small investment.

Analyze your trades after every outcome on what went correct and where there was a possibility of improvisation. Look out for market trends if you can find and match them with the crypto trade movement. There is also an option esp. if Sam decides he would essentially like to start trading, he can try it with a demo account. The demo account is easy to setup on several trading platforms, is free and does not require any time-consuming verification processes. The trading carried out through demo accounts is the same as it would be carried out in reality and thus, it is an excellent way to develop your trading strategy and understand the movement of the market. This also helps in witnessing the impact of any news or announcements having an impact on the crypto market.

b) **Understand your 'gains':** Tom stressed extremely hard on this point. If someone encounters a loss on his first invest he would directly make an analysis on what went wrong and improvise or leave the trading market. That's the sad reality unfortunately, that trading is not for anyone and everyone as most traders end up losing money. The bigger watch out to be aware and extremely cautious of is something called **beginners luck**. While starting small and making your first crypto trade, there might be a case that you might be in all green for the first few trades and this trend might continue for a while making you pump in more money.

This is where there needs to be a pause where any 'Sam' should understand on why he had these winning trades and does it contribute to a working strategy. He can very well do this by correlating this to market trends or any rational he had used to take a decision on a certain trade and see if this strategy is reproducible.

Beginners luck can be very challenging and sometime be worse than a first-time washout as this gets a certain level of overconfidence. Once this comes in, the crypto market becomes even more enticing and then the crypto market being volatile knock you down even harder as it had taken you forward. If you do not have a proper understanding of you 'reds' and more importantly your 'greens', then there would be a point where this might turn into a bloodbath resulting into a big loss in investment and gains.

c) **Maintain a 'portfolio' of crypto assets:** There is a very famous saying which is extremely valid for cryptocurrency investing i.e. 'Don't put all your eggs in one basket'. This saying is so true for crypto trading as well. Due to the market volatility and new cryptocurrencies coming up almost every day, it is always advisable to have a portfolio of investments in several currencies. It is very hard to predict which currency would be the next Bitcoin, or it might be that Bitcoin remains the market leader but where the cryptocurrency market would be in the next couple of years is anyone's guess.

Cryptocurrencies keep on going up and down and unless you are extremely confident about the prospects of a cryptocurrency being the game changer, having a spread would help in maximize profits and minimize loss. There are many videos on the internet where there are expert analyst predicting a crypto boom almost every second week and at the same time, there are similar videos calling out this technology as a bubble. This is the case with every new technology that there is always a certain level of uncertainty with it about its future and growth. Therefore, it is important to make an informed decision based on knowledge about the underlying technology, the challenges it is trying to solve and not get blown away by the many experts predicting the future of cryptocurrencies.

d) **Learn when to get out:** Most people know when to get in and the best time to get in is always 'now', of course if you are convinced of riding the crypto wave. The most important part is realizing when to get out. Don't ride your ego. There might be a time when you might make some money from a bull run in the market but there might also be the opposite when you lose from a bearish run during a crash.

To avoid losses from a crash you need to decide to be satisfied with a certain amount of profit you generate and accept a certain amount of loss. When the markets turn against your favor, you need kill your trades and accept a loss rather than waiting just in 'hope' of the market return which can cause a liquidation of all your trading assets in margin trading. Don't be greedy, be realistic, have a plan and make the most out of the crypto market.

e) **The loss strategy:** As there is never a fine line to decide when to get out from the market turning against you, having a sound strategy is needed to avoid a disaster. The fluctuations in the crypto market can be huge and human emotions coupled with a hope of making it big is the perfect formula for disaster. What's needed is to stay disciplined and stick to your own strategy. A strategy for loss minimization could be to decide that I would close my current position if it falls below a 10% loss and close it at a profit of 20 %. Anther strategy could be to close out all open positions at the end of the day and see how the value of my trades are shaping up in my portfolio. There is no perfect strategy but sticking to your own method is important and to learn from your mistakes on the trading patterns.

This comes through experience and it is always advisable to start trading through a demo account first until you make some money rather than going into full blast into trading with real money. There might be a day when your trades are all in red and you were 100% certain of the markets moving in your favor. At this point is hard to swallow a loss and the mind often prompts you to keep on hanging on in hope that the markets will bounce back and you will minimize your losses or maybe even make some profit. Not sticking to your strategy would be futile one day and can cause liquidation of all your assets. There is no perfect approach to a strategy while trading cryptos, but the best strategy is having one and sticking to it for a certain (planned) period.

f) **Trade the money you are willing to lose unless you are a millionaire:** The crypto market is extremely volatile and as advised start small, get a feeling of the market and then put in your money. Still, the market is extremely unpredictable and even the most informed, planned analysis could accidently result in a loss. Therefore, to avoid any regret, trade the money you are willing to lose.

In the end, it is not gambling but if you do not place educated bets, it might be nothing short of it too! Learn, trade, learn more and make the most of this new technological development. For the beginning, park the Lamborghini in your thoughts and this might come one day but would need lots of concentrated efforts and of course quite some luck!

Sam's list of key crypto terms

Account Liquidation: Complete/ partial loss of assets in a trading account while margin trading. This happens when the value of losses are higher than the available value of the account.

Altcoins: Altcoins are alternative coins or cryptocurrencies apart from Bitcoin

Bearish market: A market going down i.e. losing value is a bearish market

Bitcoin wallets: Wallets store the private key through which funds can be accessed. A Bitcoin wallet stores the private key holding Bitcoin as assets.

Bitcoin: A peer top peer digital currency developed on the Blockchain network.

Blockchain forks: Network divergent across the Blockchain network which breaks down the Blockchain into two or more parts. These generally carry out feature upgrades on the Blockchain network

Blockchain: A decentralized and distributed digital public ledger which stores data in the form of 'blocks' of information linked to the previous block thus forming a chain of such blocks.

Bullish market: A market going up i.e. gaining value is called a Bullish market

Candlestick (trading): Fundamental blocks of trading which show the market patterns

Digital signature: Data security is maintained on a Blockchain network through a Digital signature which secure transactions and ensure their authenticity

Github: World's leading software development platform

Hardware wallet: These wallets store the private keys offline and connect to the internet only during carrying out transactions, eg Trezor etc.

Hash power: The number of calculations the available hardware can perform per second to solve the mathematical puzzle, enabling transactions to be appended to the Bitcoin network

ICO's: Digital assets sold by companies based on a Blockchain network

KYC's: Know your consumer, a verification process enabled by many cryptocurrency exchanges to prevent money laundering

Margin trading: Trading on several times the money you have. The profits could be larger but at the same times the losses could be extreme too

Nonce: A cryptographic mechanism used to make blocks secure in a Blockchain network

Private coins: Cryptocurrencies which keep the details of the transactions anonymous

Private key: The private key helps users to secure their account and should not be shared with anyone

Public key: A digital address on the Blockchain is comprised of a public key which is accessibly to anyone and helps in carrying out transactions

Smart contracts: Decentralized, self-executing contracts, specifying a certain if-then condition on a Blockchain network are called as Smart contracts

Software wallet: These wallets store the private keys online through a service provider such as Coinbase.

Token air drop: A strategy used by ICO'S to give away free tokens to investors to drive mass adoption

Two factor authentications: A double verification method for securing accounts on several cryptocurrencies, enabled by Google

Sam's list of useful websites/links for further learning and tracking crypto trends

a) Cryptonews.com

b) Bitcoin.com

c) Cryptocompare.com

d) Coindesk.com

e) Ccn.com

f) News.Bitcoin.com

g) Blockchainnews.com

h) Bitcoinwiki.org

i) Cointelegraph.com

j) Bitcoin.org

k) Lisk.io

l) Coinmarketcap.com

My crypto watch out list

Below, create a list of your favorite cryptocurrencies/ICO's and keep a track about their performance through websites such as **coinmarketcap.com**

1)

2)

3)

4)

5)

If you liked the book and would encourage the author to educate the many other Sam's out there, route in your contribution the crypto way. Just scan the barcode below and find the BTC transfer key, try out your new crypto skills!

BTC only!

If you need further help in setting up a crypto portfolio, drop a note on 'whatisbitcoin@protonmail.ch'

www.ingramcontent.com/pod-product-compliance
Lightning Source LLC
Chambersburg PA
CBHW051316220526
45468CB00004B/1365